My Life
Before and After
Jesus Christ

My Life
Before and After
Jesus Christ

J. Christ

My Life Before and After Jesus Christ
Copyright © 2019 by J. Christ. All rights reserved.

No part of this publication may be reproduced, stored in a retrieval system or transmitted in any way by any means, electronic, mechanical, photocopy, recording or otherwise without the prior permission of the author except as provided by USA copyright law.

The opinions expressed by the author are not necessarily those of URLink Print and Media.

1603 Capitol Ave., Suite 310 Cheyenne, Wyoming USA 82001
1-888-980-6523 | admin@urlinkpublishing.com

URLink Print and Media is committed to excellence in the publishing industry.

Book design copyright © 2019 by URLink Print and Media. All rights reserved.

Published in the United States of America

ISBN 978-1-64367-872-6 (Paperback)
ISBN 978-1-64367-871-9 (Digital)

09.10.19

INTRODUCTION

IN 1999 I WAS HIT BY A CAR AND DIED THREE TIMES, WHEN I WAS HIT MY LIFE WAS SEX DRUGS AND ROCK N ROLL SO I ALWAYS TOLD PEOPLE WHEN I DIE AND GO TO HELL I'M GOING TO GRAB THE DEVIL BY THE HORNS AND TAKE OVER HELL. SO THE LAST TIME I DIED I OPENED MY EYE'S AND I

J. Christ

WAS IN A ROUND LAVA ROCK ROOM AND THE FEELING IN THE ROOM WAS EVIL AND VERY VERY LONELY I TRYED TO KICK THE WALL DOWN AND GET OUT BUT I COULDN'T DO IT AND WHEN I KICKED IT THE MOST EVIL LAUGH I EVER HEARD IN MY LIFE STARTED LAUGHING AT ME AND WHEN I HEARD IT I GOT GOOSE BUMPS ON MY BONES THAT CAME THRU MY SKIN I CRYED OUT OHH MY GOD AND THAT'S WHEN I KNEW WHAT TO DO. I FELL DOWN ON MY KNEE'S AND CRYED OUT TO GOD TO SAVE ME AND HE DID.AND WHEN I OPENED MY EYE'S THREE AND A HALF SECONDS LATER I WAS BACK IN MY BODY BUT IT WAS

THREE AND A HALF MONTH'S SINCE I WAS HIT AFTER I CAME BACK ALIVE I GAVE MY HEART AND SOUL TO JESUS CHRIST.

CHAPTER 1

My name is J. Christ. I was born on 02/28/1963 in Los Angeles California and I grew up in Pasadena I was about nine years old when I got my first taste of a cigarette one of my older brother's said it would taste good so I tryed it and thought it was cool. I smoked them for forty years I also did a lot of drugs any I could get my hands on and I did those everyday except when I was in jail.

Well thru my life of sex drugs and rock n roll I experienced a lot of things good and bad mostly bad. In my younger years of life living at home with my Mom and Dad I learned about Jesus Christ but I thought I didn't need him to be happy? So I went about my life of Sex Drugs and Rock n Roll. Well after about 25 years of that me and my last wife Micki was pushing our first daughter Bethany down the street in her stroller one evening. And where we was at there was no sidewalks just dirt and the street. So at first we was in the street but I told her I would help push so we crossed our fingers together on the handle and got out of the street and pushed. She kept trying to come out into the street and I kept pushing her back out of it well after a few times of that I finally told her get out of the street more because if anyone is going to be hit it was going to be me. And about five minutes later a drunk driver came along and hit me! And when he hit me my left foot was turned all the way around backwards and pushed up against my leg and I flew over the hood of his car and hit the windshield with my head at about 85 mph. And by the time I hit the street I was dead. My girlfriend Micki tried to chase the car and get the license plate number of the car but couldn't it had no light and it sped away. So she came back to see how me and Bethany was doing? I was laying in the street Bethany was in her stroller asleep. She knelt down besides me and put my head in her lap and was brushing my hair out of my face when she seen a tear drop run down my face and that's when she knew I was dead. She was in shock and crying. The people who's house we was in front of called the Cop's and Fire Department and Ambulance so they all showed up with lights and siren's blaring but she never heard or seen them. So when they got there and seen what happened they got Bethany out of her stroller and took her into the ambulance and made sure she was ok and by the grace of GOD she was so they put her back. And then they asked the cops to get Micki away from me cause she was still holding my head in her lap. So the cop got her in a bear hug and told her she needed to let the paramedic's see how I was doing. So they put her in a police truck and the paramedic's got to me and I was dead they gave me the shock thing and brought me back alive. When they was ready to take me to the Hospital they loaded me into the ambulance and they told the Police to tell

Micki I probably wouldn't make it. And then we got on the way to the hospital. Well on the way I Died again and got another shock thing and made it to the hospital where I died again. And this time I opened my eye's.

CHAPTER 2

When I opened my eyes I looked around and what I saw was lava rock all around me I was in a round lava rock room. And it was hard for me to stand up straight I kept falling to my left side so I looked down at my leg and about four inches above my ankle my foot was turned all the way around and pushed up against my leg and it didn't hurt so for a second I thought it was a dream? And in all the bad dreams I had growing up when ever anything tryed to get me or hurt me I wouldn't let it happen I became tuff and would kick there butt's and not let them hurt me I was strong also. So I figured if it was a dream I could kick the wall and get out? Well I tryed to kick it and get out but nothing happened. So I hit it with everything I had rock flew everywhere but it didn't break enough to get out and right after I hit it I heard the most horrible evil laugh I have ever heard in my life. It was so horrible and evil it made my bones get goosebumps on them that came thru my skin and when I seen them I wiped them off and instantly they came back cause the laugh never stopped laughing. So I got to thinking that lava rock is made from the hottest fire on the planet volcano's and if you fall into one poof your whole body teeth and all are gone. So I knew I wasn't knocking on heaven's door I was knocking on hell's door and the laugh was the devil's cause when I was alive in my sex drug's and rock n roll life when I'd be drunk I'd tell people when I die and go to hell I'm going to take over hell. Yeah right like that cold ever happen. And then I heard the laugh again and the goosebumps came back I wiped them off a second time and poof they was back again so I tryed wiping them off again and when I did I said ohh my GOD!!!! That's when I knew what I had to do? I feel down on my knee's and bowed my head and cryed out to GOD PLEASE TAKE ME BACK? I wanted to go back to see if my daughter and girl friend was ok? I asked if he would take me back just for a second so I could see if they was ok I'd come back and stay there for how ever long he wanted me to? Well I was in that room for about three and a half second's and when I opened my eye's from praying I was back in my body and it was three and a half

J. Christ

month's since I'd been hit by the car. And the first thing I saw was a green slimy tube flying thru the air and it feel on the floor and hit some guys shoe. Well I was thinking what the heck was that and where did it come from? So after that I tried to get up and I couldn't cause I was strapped down to a bed so I looked around thinking where the heck am I at now? And what I saw when I looked around I was in an ambulance and there was a door and I thought my girlfriend and daughter must be on the other side of that door? So I tryed to stand up and get to the door so I could open it and see if they was out there and if they was ok? Well I couldn't get up I was strapped down so I took off some of the straps and sat up. And when I did that the guy who the slimy tube hit his shoe pushed me down. And he had that slimy tube in his hand and he was trying to put it in my mouth. Well

I wasn't having none of that I knocked it out of his hand and said dude what do you think your doing? I mean man look at that thing it's all slimy and nasty and was on the floor up against your foot your not putting that thing in my mouth I'm out of here. And then I leaned forward to undo the last strap and all of a sudden it felt like I was asleep again? And it felt like I was dreaming again? I kind of woke up because I was in pain!!!! It felt like every hair on my stomach was being pulled all at the same time. Well in my mind I thought there was a bunch of little Devil's on my stomach pulling my hair because of where I was at before with the Devil laughing at me. I opened my eye's and looked at my stomach to see if there was a bunch of Devil's pulling my hair and there wasn't Thank GOD. But what I saw was what looked like a big worm wrapped up in my hair and every time I took a breath it pulled all my hair at one time. Well the first thing that came to my mind was a Alfred Hitchcock movie I seen when I was nine years old and the song at the beginning went (The worms crawl in the worms crawl out in your stomach and out your mouth.) Well I thought to my self ohhh nooo your not coming out my mouth? So I grabbed it and pulled it out it and it made a loud pop sound when it came out and I looked at it and it had teeth on both end's it had rubber ones on the end that was in my stomach and metal ones on the outside of my stomach so I thought man this thing was eating me from the inside out? Well I seen a trashcan and threw it away and looked around and thought where was I at now?

CHAPTER 3

Well when I looked around the room after throwing away the worm I noticed I was in some kind of Hospital triage room or that's what it looked like? And I felt real hungry so I looked around the room to see if there was by chance some food? Well I looked across the room and saw a bag from taco bell soon as I seen it I heard Angels singing and I started praying to GOD asking him when I get to the bag to please let there be something to eat in it a tub of hot sauce of ketchup or something? And not to let there be a bunch of trash in it like I've done before after eating out somewhere like that put all my trash in the bag and leave it ya know? Well when I jumped off the bed I fell down on my knees cause it felt like my left foot was gone because I couldn't feel it!!! I looked down praying please let it be there? It was there thank GOD I just couldn't feel it I thought ok it must be asleep so I got up and limped over to the bag praying all the way for there to be something to eat in it? With my eye's closed and praying I grabbed the bag and picked it up and it was heavy and I heard angels singing again but louder this time so I limped back to my bed praying all the way for a tub of hot sauce or ketchup and when I got to my bed I sat down closed my eye's praying again for something to eat be in the bag instead of a bag of trash? So with my eye's closed I opened the bag and finished praying and when I opened my eye's and looked into the bag I heard trumpet's drum's and angels singing real loud cause there was a chimichanga burrito in the bag I thanked GOD for it and it disappeared in a second into my mouth. that was the best burrito I've ever ate in my life. I wiped my mouth and hands off real good threw the napkins away rolled the bag back up like it was when I found it and put it back on the table and got back into bed cause I figured well if that wasn't my burrito who's ever it was might be back looking for it? And a few minutes later a nurse opened the door took one step looked at me and Froze in place and got a real stern look on her face and told me you ate my burrito!!! I said no I didn't! But she kept saying yes you did I kept saying no I didn't. I wasn't confessing to nothing. So she walked over to the bed and when she got to the bed she raised her hand and I thought she was gong to bipp me up side the head so I put my hands up to block her. She say's what you doing? I said blocking you so you don't bipp me upside the head? She says I'm not going to bipp you upside your head I want to show you something? I was yeah right sure you are? She convinced me to let her show me what she wanted to show me and she wiped my chest and showed me guacamole sauce and there was a lot of it to. I thought to my self man how did I get so much of it down there? So I felt down there to see exactly how much was there? And there was a lot. But I also felt something hard on my neck and not knowing what it was I pulled it off. Well the nurse turned white as a ghost and couldn't talk all she could do is say mmmmmrrrrrr Pearson ohhhh mmmmrrr Pearson and she turned around and out the door she went quickly I yelled hey where you going got anymore burritos? Well she was gone out the door. So I looked at the thing I pulled off my neck and it was hard plastic I couldn't figure out what it was so I threw it away and layed back to watch T.V and hope she was going to bring me another burrito? Ok another five minute's went by and the door opened again but this time it was the nurse and some guy who had a bag of oatmeal in his hand. He went behind me and hung it up on the IV pole thing and was leaning over me. That's when I said hey what are you doing back there? He say's I'm looking for your feeding tube? I said looking around what's a feeding tube? He say's it should be in my stomach? I go ohhh you mean the worm? His and the nurse's eye's got real big and they shook there heads and go worm? I said yeah I threw that away. He looks at the nurse like go see if it's in the trash? So she go's to the trash can and looks down into it and starts rocking her head back and forth and looks up with a grin on her face and says yup. They couldn't believe I pulled it out? So now he had another one of those plastic thing's I pulled of my neck in his hand and say's OK well let me put this thing back on? That's when I said wait a minute who are you? Where am I? And where's my girl friend and daughter at? Well he say's your at a rehabilitation Hospital cause you was hit by a car. And he told me my girl friend and daughter was dead! Cause my Mom didn't like my girl friend and she took out a conservatorship on me so she could tell the doctors what kind of medicine's to give me and to keep my girlfriend away from me. Well I told them they was out of there minds cause I knew they was Ok cause I made sure of it. And I wanted to use a phone so I asked them where was one at? They said it was down the hall. Well I jumped up and was headed out the door when they started to panic and ask me to get into a wheelchair and they would take me to it cause they was afraid I would fall because of my leg so I got into the wheelchair and we went out the door and down a hallway. When we got to the end of the hallway the phone was to the right of us and the front door was in front of us and soon as we got to that point of the hallway and I could see the door it opened and guess who walked in? You guessed it my girlfriend did. I jumped up out of that wheelchair and was headed to her side when I went past a wall where some big guard was at, And just as I got past it he grabbed me in a bear hug and says where do you think your going? Well I was kicking and cussing let me go I'm going with her!!!! He says no your not we've called the cops on her and you have to stay here. Well when she heard cops she was gone out the door I would of done the same thing. So I was mad and told them to take me out back so I could smoke and they had me get back in the wheelchair so they could take me to go smoke. Well little did they know I was hoping we would get there before her and the guy she got a ride from would get out the driveway and be gone? Well soon as we got outside I seen the truck turning out to the street. So I sat back and smoked my cigarette and talked to the nurse for a while. When I was done we went back inside to see if I could get something else to eat? They took me to the cafeteria to get something else to eat. Well when we got there they had some burrito's but they was small as a school burrito they would only give me two of them cause I ate the nurse's. I told them I was starving two wont be enough for me I need at least six of those dinky thing's. Well they gave me five and said that's all I could have. So I ate them in like a minute and went and smoked again. And went back to my room and watched some cartoon's. (I know what your thinking why is a grown man watching cartoons right?) Well I love me some cartoons bugs bunny and daffy duck. So I was there for about I remember three weeks or so not to sure? But all I wanted to do was get out of there to see my girl friend and daughter. So on the day I got out I had to go with my Mom cause she had the conservatorship on me. So I tryed to get her to take me to where my girlfriend and daughter was at but she wouldn't she took me to my old girlfriend's house and left me there. Well I didn't want to be there so I found me a ride to my Moms house cause that's where I had to stay for the time being. And while I was there after a month or so my girlfriend came over and I tryed to get in the car with her and leave however, the person who's auto it was wouldn't let me with him cause my mother let him know if he did she would have him arrested so I had to stay and I did for the time being again but I told her I would call her the next day and we would work something out to where I would come with her so we could be together she said OK and left. Well the next day when everyone was gone I went to the phone and called her and told her I was home alone to come up and get me right away. She says OK she had some friends who could come up and get me. Well they came up and I got in the car with them and we left to go to where she was at. When we got there all I could do is cry cause I was so happy so we spent about three days together me her and our daughter. When on the third day there was a knock on the door and one of the other people who was there answered the door and all I heard was cops! Well I tryed to hide but there was no where to hide so I just went out to see what they wanted? Well it was my Mom sister and the cops wanting me to go home with them. So they took my girlfriend cause of some issues. So I grabbed my daughter and said I'm staying here with her. Well I haven't found out about the conservatorship thing until now when the cops told me I had to go with my Mom because of it and if I didn't go they was going to take me to jail? Well I was for all that cause it meant I could sit next to my girlfriend on the way to jail cause there was only one cop car? And I've been to jail before so I wasn't afraid to go. So when they figured that out they threatened to take me to the nuthouse. And I told them let's go cause I've never been there before and I've heard a lot of story's about it made me wonder what it would be like? And I knew that soon as I got there I would be let go cause I wasn't crazy. So the cops told me look man if you go home with your Mom now we wont arrest you. So I was thinking if I got into the car with them and the cops left I could get back out of the car and stay there with my daughter? Well when they came to a stop sign I tryed to jump out of the car so they wouldn't go they yelled at me to close the door and tryed to drive away well when we got to the freeway Onramp they stopped and I tryed to get out again they tryed to take off again. But then they parked the car and I jumped out and was heading back down the road to be with my daughter when I looked down the street and right behind us was the cops they got on there loud speaker and told me to come over to there car? Well I did and they asked me what the heck was I doing? I told them I didn't want to leave my daughter there by her self and they said there was nothing they could do about that. But they did say if I would just go home with my Mom and sister that if soon as we pulled in the yard I jumped out and headed back down there and they called them again they wouldn't come out. So I agreed with them and went with them. The following day I called down where my little girl was at to see how she was doing the person said she was doing fine and that my better half would be out there in a day so I disclosed to them a debt of gratitude is in order for helping us and hung up. In three day's she was out finally. When I called to see how our daughter was doing so I told her to come up and get me again that night and then we would hideout and be together and she did and we was and no one found us until we wanted them to.

Well about two or three month's went by before we told any of our family where we was at. We had gotten an apartment and was living there for a while and then we heard about my sister trying to find out where I was at so we called her and told her so she could come over and see us. It was our daughter Beth's one year birthday and my sister wanted to bring a cake and her kids over for her birthday so I told her where we lived at so she could bring her kids over. She brought a cake and We had a great time watching Beth eating the cake with her fingers she was a mess but she loved it and so did we. So now everyone knew where we was at but nothing came of it they left us alone. After we left the apartment we went and lived with some friends where we got back into the drugs and we stayed there for a few months. And after we left there we went to Louisiana for a month and when we got back we did the same thing again back into the drugs and stayed in motels for a few months and after the few months they wouldn't let us stay there anymore so we had nowhere to go. So I remembered some friends of ours who we used to sell and buy drugs from had a house. And I thought if we got some drugs we could go over there and share with them if they would let us stay until the first of next month which was about a week or two away? When we got there and knocked on the door she was home and she let us in. And we talked for a bit and asked her how everything was going with her and her husband and kids? She said all was great. That's when I asked her if we could stay till the first of next month and if so we would give her some of our drugs we had? She said she didn't want any drugs cause her and her husband didn't do them anymore because they had given there life's to JESUS CHRIST But she said we could stay and our kids could stay in the room with her kids and me and my girlfriend could stay out back in a camper they had if we promised we would go to a Church camp for people who needed help so we said yeah we would go. So the next day she gave my girlfriend a ride to the women's camp and took me to the Church where they would give me a ride to the men's camp. And when I got there I was thinking ok we will stay here till the first and then we would go to Church and leave and get our welfare check and go find a place to stay and get some drugs. Well GOD had a better idea. And we stayed there for about a month and a half. One morning while at Church I was wanting to go smoke because when I got there the ride

I was with got there late so they wouldn't let me go have a smoke. Well that made me mad. So while I was waiting for Church to start I was talking to another guy who was mad to and wanted to go smoke and I wasn't paying attention cause I wanted to go smoke. Well my girlfriend she was paying attention and she took my hand and started pulling me thru the sanctuary and I thought we was going to go smoke? Well I told the guy see ya later I'm going to smoke? Well that's what I thought we was doing but when we got to about the middle of the sanctuary we stopped. Well soon as we stopped I started listening to what the Preacher was saying and he was asking if there was anyone who wanted to accept Jesus Christ as there personal Lord and Savior and when I looked at my girlfriend she had tears coming out of her eyes like a water hose and there was a glow all around her and right at the very second I saw that tears of pure joy was coming out of my eyes cause the glow was all around me and I could feel the LOVE OF GOD. So I accepted JESUS CHRIST on that day and have been living my life with and for him everyday since then. Well we stayed there for a few more days. And after that we got blessed out to a couples house where they tried to get us jobs and get us started on our new life with JESUS CHRIST. Rich and Rubie let us stay with them for a few months and while living there we met a couple who had a car and could get us a ride to the store. And the guy knew a women who was a realtor who we could do odd jobs for and make a few bucks. Well after a few weeks we learned about a house we could rent from her so we moved out and lived there with them for a few month's and then we found out the landlord sold the house out from under us and the new landlord wanted us to move out by the next month which was in about a week. Well we thought about where we could go for a few days when my girlfriend said we could maybe go to Houston Texas and live with her Aunt maybe? So she called her Aunt and asked her if we could come down there and stay with her for a while until we could find a job for her and then save some money and get a place of our own? And when she talked to her Aunt and asked her if we could come down her Aunt said she would have to ask her boyfriend and to call back the next day and then she would let us know? After two days she called back and talked to her Aunt and she said her boyfriend said we could come down so we made plans and moved down there with her Aunt. And after about a month of looking for a job she found one at a animal hospital. And after a few month's

I finally won my SSI case and got enough money to buy us a house and furniture to fill it with. And we moved in our new house and while living there in our new house in Houston Texas I had a few family member's passed away. First one to pass away was my older brother and I had to go to California for his funeral and I spent a week there with family and friends. And after a week I went home to Houston Texas. Every morning I lived in Texas when I got up and got kids to school and my girlfriend to work I would call my Mom and we would talk. So the very next day I got home from the funeral I called my Mom and we talked. And after a few minute's of talking to my Mom she asked me where I thought my brother went? And right when I said well I found my self in pitch black darkness I couldn't even see my hand in front of my face. So after I couldn't see my hand I prayed and asked GOD what was happening? Right after I asked that I felt something above me and when I looked up I saw the most wonderfully beautiful loving light I ever seen in all my life. It was so beautiful and when it touched me I could feel pure love coming off it and on the edge of it was my brother. Well when I seen him I asked him what he was doing up there? He said to tell my Mom he was OK. I said you come and tell her and I'll come up there and help you down to go do it. And while I was talking he got loud and told me to tell my Mom he was OK. I said no come on and I took a step toward him but soon as I took the step I was back in my chair. I was kind of shocked and wondering what just happened?

OK now I was back in my chair in disbelief of what just happened? And sitting there trying to gather my senses and figure out where I was at now? I heard a noise that sounded like Alvin and the Chimp monks, Looking around I noticed I was in my chair again and I looked outside and seen a squirrel running around and that's when I noticed the phone in my hand. And I didn't remember who was on the phone so I put it up to my ear and said hello who's this? Well it was my Mom she says what do you mean who's this? It's your Mother. She ask me where did I go? I asked her how long was I gone? She said about five to ten minutes? Well that's when I started crying and telling her where I went and what happened when I was there she started crying to we cryed for a few minutes and I was asking her why did she think GOD would show me that and not her? And she said that GOD use's the most unusual people to show his LOVE by giving them gift's to use to share with the world. So I'm sharing my story with everyone I can. And a few years later my niece passed away and when my sister Peggy called me at two am Texas time and she told me Jennifer was with the LORD we both was crying I prayed for her and her kid's to be comforted with GOD'S GRACE. And after we hung up the phone I was in my bed crying and praying for them some more. And then all of a sudden I was on the edge of HEAVEN again. But this time my Brother Jimmy was still on the edge of HEAVEN and in front of me just a few feet away there was an ANGEL and a little girl the ANGEL was gigantic about nine feet tall four feet wide with big wings and the little girl was holding his pinky and her fingers could hardly go around it. So looking at the girl I thought to my self wow that looks like Jennifer? Because she had brown hair but this girl had a lot of hair when Jennifer was here she didn't have a lot of hair and her teeth was like shark teeth and the pupil's of her eyes where shaped like cat's eyes. So while I was looking at the back of this little girl she had long wavy brown hair so I thought it was Jennifer so I called out her name and when she turned around it was her but she had beautiful long hair and she smiled at me and her teeth and pupils where perfect I thought to my self well I must get to go now? So I took one step towards her and soon as I took the step I was back in my bed crying so I thanked GOD for showing me her and cryed why did he show me this again? Well I went on with my life and a few more years later my Grandma passed away this time it was ten in the morning when my mom called me and told me she was with JESUS CHRIST so we cryed a little bit and I prayed for her and everyone who was there in California for comforting and we hung up and I had to go to the bathroom and take a crap so I went to the bathroom and got on the toilet and was still praying for everyone out there and right in the middle of taking a crap I was back at the edge of heaven and there was Jennifer and my Brother Jimmy at the edge of heaven and this time there was another or maybe the same ANGEL but with him was an older Lady and I figured it must be my Grandma because I was just told she passed away so I said hey Grandma and she turned around and it was my Grandma but she didn't have anymore wringle's cause when she passed away she was in her ninity's and had wringle's on her face but now she didn't I knew she had a new body like it says in the Bible 2Corinthians 5:1 - 10 Revelation 21:1-4 NLT is where you can find it at if you would like to know exactly what it talks about when we die and go to Heaven. MY

J. Christ

PRAYER EVERYDAY IS FOR ALL THE WORLD TO KNOW AND EXCEPT JESUS CHRIST AS THERE PERSONAL LORD AND SAVIOR GOD BLESS EVERYONE ALWAYS AMEN!!!!!!!!!!!!!!!!!!!!!!!

www.ingramcontent.com/pod-product-compliance
Lightning Source LLC
LaVergne TN
LVHW021741060526
838200LV00052B/3402